How to build your way to

Financial Immunity

By K.D. Brew

Grow Your Health and Wealth in 90 days

Acknowledgements

Your life is all about your experiences and your encounters. I've been fortunate enough to be blessed with a pretty extraordinary life. I want to acknowledge the people who add to my every day strength.

My Strength and My Loves

My children Jesse, Cameron, June

My Aunties, My homies Yolanda and my Aunt Ronay

My Parents and my sisters and brothers, I love you, I hope you all know that

My BFF's GT, and Gracie

My Spiritual advisor and My Friend B Long

My Facebook Besties: Quanyell and Tribeca

To all my family I couldn't possibly name you all but from the bottom of my heart I wish I could

I wish I could name all my Facebook friends that love and inspire me daily but you all know who you are.

My biggest shout out goes to my son Jesse because without you son, none of this would have even been possible. You are my son, my moon and my stars.

All of you have added to my Greatness as a person and I am forever grateful.

#GOLIFECOACH

In loving memory of my Grandmother Viola Davis,

I know you're with me every step of the way

Rest in Power

Contents

Immunity Quick Guide
Pg. 41- 43

Preface

Today, I have spoken across the United States aiding people in developing Health and Financial Immunity. Being a part of your success is very important to me. I had to first create it for myself to prove to you it works. Your comeback story is all that matters. Life most certainly will knock you down but it's all about how you get back up. I've develop and sold many businesses and currently own and operate three. I still deliver patient care, it's just in my blood, I will always be someone who cares about people. You all have become my why in life. I always tell people don't ever worry about how you are going to do something it will, focus on why you are doing it. Focus on the why and the how will follow. This my way of giving back to the universe that has blessed me abundantly. I want to give special thanks to the Go Life Coach Family that sponsored and supported this effort 100%. Thank you for believing in me when some days I found it difficult. The seeds that you plant in life are everything. I hope this book planted a seed of inspiration to all who will read it. My intention is to make available to you the opportunity of creating stellar Health and Wealth through developing financial immunity, for not only you but also the people that you love.

Remember the World is Waiting on you because your Life Matters.

Financial Immunity: Grow your Health and Wealth in 90 days

Introduction

What is happening to our financial market? There is so much uncertainty and no one can guarantee which way the economy is going to swing. How would you like to have the benefit of not being concerned with the instability of the financial market and wondering if the down turn of the market will make or break you? We live by checking the forecast. What's the weather going to be like today, we often ask. While, the financial market also has a forecast and it looks like another storm is approaching. Financial analyst predicts a crisis happens with every Presidential election. So, it's time to do business and get to work. Doing business is always risky, but changing your mindset to the way you operate and your relationship to the way you do business must evolve to gain immunity to your external environment. Ok, now you have the book and you're probably thinking what is this, what is this all about, how is this going to happen. You know you're circumstances in life better than I do today, and it probably seems impossible to convert your health and your finances in 90 days. It seems impossible because our brains are designed to ask those questions, anytime something foreign comes into our life to invoke any type of change, whether you want the change or not. Our brains are designed to over think and trick us into over analyzing everything. It tricks us into hesitation and not moving forward. I hear people say all the time, I need more information or I need to do more research. But the funny thing is they never do the research. They just didn't have a reason to say No at the time, so the mind creates an excuse, a quick diversion. And if most of us look at our lives, we can find the excuses we gave ourselves to stop us from going after the things we wanted the most but were too afraid to act on. We often lose sight of who we are in life because our excuses have blocked us from playing full out to our full potential. This is the reason why wealth is not abundant in most of our lives. It's been said that you can't make a Billion dollars with a Fifty-thousand-dollar mind set. If you want to succeed you must study success. For years, I have studied the habits of Bill Gates, Warren Buffett, and Steve Jobs. Looking for how I can apply their strategies and mind set too my life.

Making money in a down market is possible. When the market is, volatile people become, afraid and loss happens but this is the time to strike when no one is looking. Master the art of buy low, sell high. If you hesitate you will miss the opportunity. This is one of the strategies of Millionaires, they don't wait to make decisions. They make the decision and they go with it, then they mentally support that decision by adding leverage. Your mindset is crucial to your success in granting your immunity. Let's look at your mindset knowing who you are and where you want to be is an important component. Find out who you are but don't be afraid to grow. Most people go their entire life asking who am I and what is my purpose. I use to think the same way. I use to think I was my job, not realizing, that's what I do. I use to think, I am the mother of three children and even as noble as that may seem, it doesn't give you the essence of who I am. The essence of who I am is someone who truly, deep down inside cares about people. I am passionate about my love for human life and the human experience. To be honest, we were all love, until we experienced pain, disappointment and upset and then that essence we once knew faded into the abyss and gets replaced by someone who has difficulty explaining who they are today. Think about a baby new into the world who is full of love and will go with anyone because they have no sense of danger. It's the innocence of life. As we grow we become more cynical, doubtful and afraid to take risk in so many areas of our life, we become afraid to grow. Imagine if plants were afraid to grow, we would have no life-giving food. Our past hurts and failures continually have us doubting our abilities in life. Every day we analyze our lives and wonder how did we get here. Well, it all starts with a seed. I'm not sure if we are aware of all the seeds we plant in a day. Whether it be a seed of success or doubt, it's still a seed left to flourish and grow or a seed to manifest destruction. We all want our love ones to not experience the pain that we felt in our past attempts so we often place self-limiting beliefs on them as a way of protection or we fear that they will succeed and leave us behind. I remember the day my son came to me, very excited and said Mom I have an idea for a business and I replied Really, he stated "yes and I think it's going to work". His excitement was infectious. I was eager to hear his great idea. He goes into very technical terms about, how he has an idea for launching this Website titled Go Life Coach.com. I thought wow that's a cool name and then he says and I'm going to need you to go back into the business. That's the moment I cringed. Even though I was excited for him, I wanted to ask, can't you use another business for the prototype to jump start your business. Afraid to seem unsupportive or uncooperative, I said nothing hoping that his dream would soon fade away and I would not have to reveal, that I'm not ready to go back on stage and face my fears of not having the same success I had in the past. At this point we are talking a gap of 17 years since I had last been on the big stage. It's like bringing those old has been out of retirement and asking them to win the Super bowl. You reminisce about the days, when you were the man on top. Just to give you some background when my son was a toddler, I went into the self-help industry seeking to make sense of my life after a failed marriage. After seeing the benefits of the work, I experienced how it changed lives, I committed myself to the work of helping others to live an extraordinary life they loved. I advanced myself to becoming a well sought out Corporate Consultant, habit re-programmer, Life strategist and Transformational coach. I would get a high off seeing people achieve the impossible and making it possible in their lives. Initially I started the work on myself to seek refuge from the pain of a failed marriage, to uncovering and healing years of buried guilt and shame from my past, that may seem small to some but it was huge to me. I did the work and now was qualified and certified to aid others in their self-discovery and self-recovery from the battles of life. Life is a battlefield. Life is a Game. Life is a bowl of cherries. Life is what you make it. Life to me is all about the interpretation of how you view your own life. My motto is "Your life goes the way it goes because you say so, no one else get's the privilege of determining your life". Through all my encounters the one thing I discovered, no matter where I went or who I was being during that encounter I was a seed that was planted in the lives of many. The greatest reward you can receive is hearing the words because of you my life changed.

The Storm

Many storms have come and gone, but the storm I was in this time, who knew it would turn out to be my saving grace. There I was, holding on by my fingertips afraid to look down. All I could do to keep my balance was look up. I knew if I looked down I was doomed to fall. Paralyzed for a moment, I thought I can't do this. My son staring at me with the utmost confidence never thinking for a moment that I wouldn't be excited that he had decided to use my Life Coaching business as the prototype to kick start his business, I shuttered, thinking now is not the time. My life was a mess. At times my life seems to be a controlled well-hidden ball of turmoil. No one knew the sense of shame I felt inside. All the things I had taught my son over the years suddenly came back to haunt me. Who knew he was even listening. I couldn't use any excuses, I always taught him to never live in his excuses. I couldn't use I was afraid. I always taught him to move past his fears. So, what am I to do now? See the truth is one day I was confronted with the life I created for myself. I was surprised that all the good choices I thought I was making for myself throughout the years, would lead me to a road of Depletion, Despair, Desperation and Depression. Fighting the feelings of the 4 big D'S was bad enough but fighting while attempting to be a role model, I thought would make me come off as phony or weak, so I went into hiding. I couldn't possibly show the world that I too encounter storms. However, it's not about the storm but indeed how fast you can recover from the effects of the storm. This storm ran for about three years and at this point I was tired, exhausted and not ready to face the world. I had been in so many battles that I was barely recognizable even to myself.

Over twenty years in the field of Nursing and being life's cheerleader, I wondered how could this happen. I had given my life to benefit so many others with my gift of healing, and now I'm in need of a dose of my own medicine. I had no choice but to save myself. At this point I realized no one knew I was in trouble. At that moment, I started the process of protecting myself. One of the most vulnerable moments in life is when there is a threat to your health or to your financial resources, either through, loss of a job, theft or misappropriation of funds. One of the worst feeling in the world, is the feeling of being unprotected. I knew I needed to take steps to protect my health so that, I could be there for my children and to protect my finances, so that I could provide for them as well. I needed to build up a shield of protection to anything that could pose a threat, I needed to develop immunity. Being a Registered Nurse I am all too familiar with the benefits of immunity.

As years and years passed by I thought of those from the past and even had re-encounters with many people I helped on their path to recovery. All the seeds I had implanted in others came back to make a deposit in my life, often recanting my own words of encouragement, "You can have it now". I knew the hardest part was getting started, but I also knew action needed to be injected. That's the first step to being protected. You must do something towards being the change you want to see. So, I began to work diligently to build immunity. The wise time to act is not once you have been attacked but while you are free from any possible threat. I've coached hundreds of people but now due to social isolation I lost contact with my former coach. To be the best no matter how good you think you are, you need a coach. Michael Jordan arguably the best that ever played the game of basketball has a coach. So, I knew it would be a struggle without one. I've always had confidence in my ability to coach others. That was one thing I knew I could do. Because of my extensive training, confidence and will, I now had to save myself. I had to become my own Source. I used every tool in my arsenal to go into the battlefield with the self, myself. This is a battle that is not easily won. The storm was grounded in fear, past failures, hurt, regret, self-doubt and full of great excuses. I had to command the storm to stop, I used everything I had, but still it was resistant to stay alive in my life. It wanted to live, it wanted a purpose, it wanted to be right, wanted to win. Finally, I gave up pulling back and creating resistance. I rode the wave suddenly the winds didn't blow as hard. As my fear and anxiety subsided I began to look around and notice the old bits and pieces about myself had fell to the ground. I had been shattered. This was the best moment I could possibly experience because now I can begin to put me back together the way I want to and leave that old stuff on the ground behind me. So, now the storm has passed, the air is clear and now I can find my way. Guaranteed in life there will be storms but when you are well protected, because you acted, to creating immunity, you can rest easy. Who knew the entire time in the war against myself, that my excuses were my opposing sides best weapon against me. When I disarmed the excuses, in my life I found my results. My most powerful quote today "When you get rid of your excuses you find your results".

The Seed

The cycle of life begins with the implantation of a seed, whether it occurs in the earth, the mind or the womb, a seed must be implanted. Think of all the stages the seed must go through, to even be acknowledged and accepted for what it is soon to be.

Whether it is good or bad the seed at some point will be recognized. Let's look at the seed itself. One can implant a seed into the mind of another to flourish and give life giving properties or one can plant a seed of doubt and give death destroying properties. We must be aware of our own vulnerabilities to seeds, that are attempting to implant into our minds. It's very difficult for a seed to flourish in a toxic environment. It is possible but the seed will always struggle with not meeting the demand of its full potential. When we suspect a possible threat, we seek out a counter measure for protection. We cultivate the soil to promote growth. For a seed to grow in the womb it must be fertile. When it comes to the mind, the mind must be fertile for necessary growth, but when the mind is weak and vulnerable it is much easier for a negative thought to be implanted. Fertilizing the mind with strong properties are vital to your own growth and development. Recognizing and removing toxic people is a necessary action to building the immunity that is required. When an annual seed is planted, outside forces can occur but you can guarantee no matter what, that seed will be back next year. You must go through quite an effort to stop it from coming back. It's nature's way, to stand strong. Just when those forces thought you were down suddenly up through the darkness into the light you appear, it's apparent you were the seed that had come back to pay the return.

It's March the ideal time to plant seeds if you are growing a garden. We all know the best nutrition to receive is directly through nature. It's just natural to become aligned and in tune with nature. To grow our health, is to get back to nature. When we look at the compositions of the human body and the earth, the elements and properties are remotely the same. We look to nature to aid us in building a strong immune system. Immunity from life threatening ailments are vital to our human survival. A big topic for debate is whether to inoculate your child or not. What's not up for the debate is the benefit of immunity. We all want immunity. When your health is threatened, you will do anything to preserve your life. It's just instinct to want to protect yourself. To preserve our crops, we take action to protect the harvest which is the reward. We remove weeds (toxic people). We spray with pesticides (develop immunity). We act before the crops are affected and destroyed.

Now ask yourself if we act to protect ourselves in these other areas of our lives why are we so predisposed to the threat of illness and financial despair. One reason is lack of awareness; we don't know we need to prepare. Not being aware of the vulnerability can leave you caught off guard and susceptible to destruction. The other reason is, we don't know how to prepare. Out of identifying a need, I developed a system to assist us all, in building immunity to these potential threats. No matter what happens you will know that you took action in preparing to weather the storms ahead.

What Matters

No matter what your background, race, religion, geographical location or financial status you are, we are all susceptible to loss, no one is immune without immunity. You can take a very rich man and find him susceptible to the loss of good health and fortune. So, what made him vulnerable is not being aware that he wasn't exempt. No one is exempt without realizing you are better protected with the guard of immunity. Immunity does not mean it's not fail proof but it does mean you stand a greater chance than others without it. Steve Jobs proved that you can have wealth and still become vulnerable to health issues. It's been said, had he sought earlier treatment he would have stood a greater chance. The only chance he truly stood was avoiding death a little longer. Death is inevitable we can't avoid it. We all are looking to have the best possible experience we can possibly have during our life time. I would say Steve Jobs accomplished that as proof that he was the Innovator that changed our lives forever. He will always be remembered for his contribution to the way we operate our lives today. When it was time to take action in business, he acted. He also acted when it came to his health even though, some may say by the time he did, it was too late. If you know his story, you know he was fired from a company he helped to create. I guess we can say he didn't create immunity because he wasn't aware he had too. You must do things to establish and preserve the benefits of immunity. Meaning you must act now to create a barrier of protection to increase your survival. Not after the fact, but now, and that's the problem, we always think we have time. One day, I met a man, he told me a story of how be purchased long term disability protection one week before being gunned down and paralyzed. He went on to tell me how he battled with spending the money to protect his self because he never thought that he would need it. Luckily he took the step to provide the added benefit but never dreamed he would be cashing in so soon. The matter is simple; we need to take the time to get the added benefits in life sooner than later. We must prepare.

Now let's go back to our seed. With great excitement, we have seeds in hand and we are looking for the best place to insert our seed into the ground. We don't want to just put them anywhere. Let's remember we can plant all year around, that's not a barrier for us. We can plant in pots inside our home or outside in the yard. We have options. Next, we look to clear a space for our seeds to grown. To start we remove any barriers that will interfere with our growth, so we remove rocks, weeds (toxic people) anything that will create a hindrance. We prepare the soil using good fertilizer (positive thoughts). We watch for signs of budding through the soil (these are positive effects in our life). We look for what matters and we remove what doesn't matter around us, and seek information, we need first to grant us success, this is vital to growing a good crop to give us the results we desire. The results matter the most. The process can vary but all that matters in the end are the results.

A good friend and a former student of my coaching dropped by for a visit to my home. My son mentions to her, the idea he had for this site he wanted to create Go Life Coach.com. For the first time, I sat pretty much silent. My friend starts talking about all the life changing benefits she never dreamed could happen. She started talking about how at one time she thought a relationship her daughter would be impossible, not only was it possible but better than she could ever dreamed and is frightened to think about of the time that would have been lost without her receiving coaching. She stated "I had no idea that was on the menu. As she went on and on about how this work changed her path and gave her the courage to act in gaining financial freedom. When we started out the coaching sessions it was coaching for weight loss. In agreeing to be coached on weight loss she received not only a new a career with unlimited potential earnings and on track to making her first million ever in life but the bonus of having an unbreakable bond with her daughter but also, built immunity to the self-destructive storms of life. All the seeds I planted in my son over his lifetime had now come back to replant me. My friend came back to fertilize me, in effort to make sure I grow. Not grow tomorrow but grow today. It took a few weeks but then a bud began to emerge. In the end, all that Matters are the results.

The Threat

I'll never forget I get a call, it's the office. They needed me to come in only to my surprise I'm being fired. Ok this is my worst nightmare that turned out to be my best dream. No money saved not knowing where to go and what to do, I call my mother after balling my eye out in the car, I wipe the tears from my eyes, I knew I had to get to work. I was already tired and exhausted I needed a break. I took a deep breath and thought wow I don't have to go to work tomorrow I can sleep to late and smiled. It was income tax time I filed and realized I had 3 months' worth of resources to survive. I knew being a nurse that it wouldn't be hard to find work and since I was fired I was eligible for unemployment. The job never gave a sufficient reason for letting me go but looking back it was time for a life adjustment that I would not have been able make working a full-time job where I was underpaid and struggling. Suddenly I could breath. Now I have a relatable experience of feeling the vulnerability of a threat to my finances. During this time, I'm in school, raising my children alone and wondering what the heck is going on. Before this began I was stressed to the max working every day not having enough money to make ends meets. Working 2 other part time jobs but watching my weight sky rocket. Feeling powerless to help myself. Once I was fired I was free to go to the gym and prepare the proper meals to help me lose weight. I started to feel good about myself, which was something I hadn't felt in a long time. This is where I noticed my way was not working anymore and I needed to do something to sustain this good feeling I was feeling. I began to identify that I had left myself open to the threat of major illness. If I didn't change and change fast I would be in major trouble. I did a full body toxic focusing on all the major organs. I started practicing methods to reducing my stress levels and rebooting my immune system. Eating right and daily exercise was top priority. I started to look at my finances and how dedicating all my time to a job that could just one day easily decide to change my life circumstances was not serving me at all. I knew it was time to create immunity for myself and my family. I then began the process of clearing out my life for a new life to emerge. Top priority was living life on my terms. See, it's not so much what happened during this threat that matters, but how you react and how quickly you react to what happened, is what Matters the most.

New Creation

Suddenly, I'm noticing not only the pounds shedding but also all the heavy emotional burden I was carrying. I started to look at who I was beginning in the past which was a victim. I had given away all my power to the outside forces to control me. I was left with nothing but shame and embarrassment that this happened to me the same person that had empowered so many others and now I was left with nothing but a shell and small remembrance of who I use to be. It seemed like the day I left the big stage, I also left my confidence and power behind on that stage as well. I did things since that time on a smaller scale but nothing like being on the field in the game. Back then it was all or nothing, I was living the life that I preached. I was living an extraordinary life that I loved but where had it all gone. Dwelling in the past would only keep me stuck in the past. The only way to move forward was I had to settle the bill with my past. Looking back, it was time served in my own personal hell and today I was being released. I always taught my students the power of possibility. Creating what is possible when you are given a blank sheet of paper to write the story of your life, free from the past. Now, I was granted a new lease to create a new story. It was time I could become the hero in the story of my life and live life on my terms. But, who did I need to become to pull this off and not revert to my old ways. I created the possibility of becoming my own man. Meaning I owned being my own person and my words would define me. My word matters, I no longer look for the approval of others. I lived life on my terms and my terms alone. My life goes the way I say so. I will not accept the negative seeds attempting to implant themselves in me. I will not be limited by the belief of others. I am my own best Creation.

To Be or Not to Be

If you could be anything in the world you wanted, at the age of 50 what would it be? After careful analysis, I realized all these years I had become who I thought others wanted me to be. I decided at the age of 5 I wanted to become a nurse and my parents held me to my word. So, a five-year-old child decided what I should do with the rest of my life. If I even suggested doing something else, it was automatically shut down. Repeatedly I was instructed, finish school and if then I wanted to do something else, I could do it then. The notion during that time, was to go to college and get a good job, was a sign of success. Wealth building and owning your future through business ownership was not a conversation that was had. You became whatever your parents wanted you to be. If you didn't like it, it was too bad. I can only imagine if back then, I said to my parents I want to become a Speaker the look that would have come upon their face and soon a discussion about how I could never be such a thing. When they would say, you can be want ever you want to be that was only a catch phrase but nobody meant that. At least that's the way I remembered it. I was determined when I became a parent I would mean that catch phrase. I remember I had a similar experience with my son, because life will always test you. Although initially, the plan was for him to become an electrician, he comes to me one day and says I don't want to be an electrician, I said well what do you want to be, he said "I want to become a film director I felt my heart drop to the pit of stomach. I quickly gathered myself and thought what did Steven Spielberg parents say when he hit them with the same news. I had to remember this is not my life and I knew all too well the feeling of what it feels like when your parents control what you are destine to do for the rest of your life. Today, my son is happy on a path that he chose for himself and is experiencing the freedom to choose his own path to financially support himself. Who I chose to be in that moment was a parent that trusted their child to make the right choices for his life, free of my interception. Who I had become was someone who could trust freedom of choice. Now it was time to grant that to myself. Trust myself to make the right choices in life. This process that I'm taking you through is the same process I went through to free myself and led me to the life I have today of Financial and Health Immunity. Now, ask yourself again who could I be in this moment. A risk taker or a Procrastinator.

It's Ok to Let Go

We all have our story. Because life is full of un-expectancies, we all have a hard luck story to give. I have my story of being down and out but the story doesn't matter and quite frankly no one cares. People are looking for the result and asking how can this benefit me. We are a society of results seekers. We go on a diet one day and expect results the next day. I can't guarantee you anything unless you are willing to do the work. It's hard to let go of old ways of being and become someone new to evoke change and I get it. I offer coaching to anyone who buys my system but I want results too. When you win, I win. It's going to take hard work just like the gym you will be using muscles in your life you probably never used before. Will you be better off for it, absolutely. Remember the show Survivor and the look of relief the contestants had on their face when they were granted immunity. Imagine the relief you will feel when you realized that you have adapted those same antibodies to develop immunity in the Health and Wealth department of your life. It's ok to let go of the expectation of what you thought it would be and start a new journey, even at 50. It's always an opportunity to do better than the day before and push past who you know yourself to be. It's ok to want to be protected from the things that make us vulnerable in life. It's scary I know but what's even scarier is what would have happened if I never took action. A study conducted of common traits amongst Millionaires found, one common trait is Millionaires, ACT. Procrastination is not a part of their makeup to success. The well-known book "Think and Grow Rich " by Napoleon Hill, talks about the characteristic of Millionaire avoiding the procrastination trap. I would not have the life I have today, if I never acted on my son's request.   This is a life of letting go of the past, what others think and the fear that almost stopped me. This is a life where the past is no longer in my future. This is a life where my children can be proud of the hero I knew myself to be. This is a life where you too can be proud of the choices you make starting today. Choose you, choose freedom, choose a new path, choose to become immune.

I hate to bust your bubble

Who will ever the forget the 2008 bubble burst. I had no clue what was going on all I knew was suddenly people everywhere seemed to hit the lottery and I didn't play the number. As quickly as it came, it went in and out like a bank robber. People now were at a loss, their life saving's gone, homes in foreclosures and families displaced and homeless. Panic wide spread retirements' gone, people out of work and nobody has an answer. What I learned was every 8 years or so there is always a financial crisis or a war, one or the other, sometime both at the same time, so what is going on with our government and why aren't we covering our butt like they are. Number one, we have been trained to believe that the government has everything under control why else would we elect them. In the end the bankers were given a huge bail out and the distraught naïve American citizen was left to blame because we were told we had become to greedy. The American dream had now become a nightmare. We went from wanting the lavish life to the tiny house because the tiny house was safer. We were reduced to wanting less in life and shame on you if you wanted more. Today we place more self-limiting beliefs on ourselves than ever before. Sales of Depression and Anxiety medications increasing day by day. Today being unhappy has took on a form of a new normal. Being unhappy is a decision, to change it requires action and a belief that happiness is available to you. Anchoring your thoughts with skill is possible to change the feeling of un-happiness to happiness that any of us can do. It takes more than motivation and positive thoughts. It takes the ritual of doing self-serving things to create happiness in your life but it requires doing something. It takes converting old bad habits into good, to repetitive action, to change. We are so caught up in the feelings that are familiar to us that we forget there are others ways to be in life. Feelings will always change so never put too much stock into the way you feeling. If you find yourself to much, in the feeling mode that often leads to rash decisions, shift your thoughts to why do I want that feeling. Feeling are important because they give us insight as to what's missing in your life. Always ground your thoughts in the why. Often we fail to act in life because we are waiting for the feeling and we miss out on so many opportunities because of this. Waiting for the right feeling to come will not bring the results you are looking for, only action will. Action brings results. The results are never final and the results are the results but the results bring you closer to the goal. According, to Warren Buffet he advises to go full steam ahead when times are volatile. When everyone else is afraid to make a move that's when you play full out. Fear can be used in your favor or fear can be used against you. The key is to look at the value and ask is this made relevant to someone. Relevance is important. It's not where the stock market is but where the stock market is going to be. If people don't see relevance and value, they are not going to make a move so remember before doing any deal or making any change to your health, think is this going to add value and relevance. If it doesn't walk away and leave the feeling about it behind as well. Some people created businesses when the bubble burst and made it work to their advantage. For example, the storage business started booming because it spoke to the need of the people. If you can speak to the needs of people you can create a position of existence in the business world. Motivation speaks to the psyche for a short time, transformation speaks forever. There is a distinct difference between the two. Being a one hit wonder will not secure your immunity. Remember we are looking to create security by providing the residual effects of immunity. I found something very interesting in certain cultures Multilevel companies (MLM) fare very well in communities where it's all about cohesiveness. When growing your health and wealth utilize your communities to create immunity. Some cultures I must admit, fare more than others but it's worth it to consider. Creation of checks, balances and removing barriers will be key to your success at creating immunity. Determine your goal for 90 days but mainly focus on the why and end-result. The how does not matter. Breaking down the 90 days will help you stay focused never focus on the entire chunk of 90 days it will only overwhelm you, focus on no more than one task at hand for the week. Diversity and hedging will help you when securing Financial Immunity. Putting all your eggs in one basket is the biggest mistake ever. Putting your eggs in many baskets will never deplete your mission for gaining immunity. When securing, your health in developing immunity pay attention to everything that you put into your body if it is not serving a specific purpose to further your health ask yourself why and detach yourself of the feeling of why you want it. We are going towards a transformation. In the end, you will receive gratification but if you can't learn to live in the why, you will eventually undo all your efforts and lose your immunity.

The Dreamer verse the Visionary

Today, as a Life Coach, I have helped hundreds of people develop Health and Financial Immunity. Someone would complain and say all you people do worry about is money. Citing things like money is the root to all evil. No not having money is the root to the evils of theft and deception. If we all had an abundance of money no one would ever use that line as a crutch to stand on. The truth is we live in a world of the have and have nots. We all live within the same 24-hour framework of society. It's what you chose to do with your 24 hours is what separates us all. Whether we chose to take act or lay in the bed is where we are left to wonder why some don't act when necessary. Some will go beyond where others stop and claim a spot in the world of being extraordinary. Most people weren't born with extraordinary qualities they were developed. When you use the excuse that someone has extraordinary qualities that you don't have, it's an excuse to keep you with self-limiting belief about yourself. We have far too many millionaires and billionaires to use the excuse of, I didn't go to college or come from a good home or money. When you look at these extraordinary individuals these were people who defied the odds and went on to being deemed extraordinary. They became visionaries and not dreamers. Dreamer do nothing but dream. Visionaries act. The reason I titled this book Financial Immunity and not Health and Financial immunity is because without having your financial health being intact your physical health is in jeopardy. At that point it's just hit or miss. Once you have developed financial immunity you are free, clear and immune to the economic changes you were once susceptible too. It is often said you are nothing without your health which is true, but without the proper finances it is difficult to manage a better health. Having access to clean water, clean food, and a holistic health support team makes managing your health a lot easier. When you are confronted with issues around your money and health, it's a scary time for us all. Without immunity, you are in your most vulnerable state. When you become recession proof it doesn't matter if the economy is up or down, you are secure. When you are secured in your wealth department, you can eat better foods, reduce and eliminate stress or at least create the ability to cope and relieve stress. You can seek better health treatments. You can protect your assets. You stand a greater chance at repositioning your economic status when you position yourself for immunity. The goal is to develop immunity.

Your Results

Your results depend solely on you. You can put this book down and never act and stay in the same position or you can take the path less traveled to gaining all the benefits to health and financial immunity. Gaining a life coach is crucial because it inserts accountability. A good life coach has a high level of integrity and proven results, not just all talk and great advice you can get that from a friend. Your results are important because it's the bar that's measured. We want you to get the results you are looking for. Now that the seed is planted, identify the why of the seed. Why do you need this is your life? Don't worry about how it's going to happen. When you establish the why the how will appear. The why will get you through the storms you will encounter, so make sure it's a strong enough why because it will be tested. Next create the possibility. Create a to-be list. Look at who you need to become for this to happen in your life. With each barrier and storm, who you need to become will become amplified. If your vision does not scare the pants off you, it's not big enough. Your vision should be bigger than you, and what you perceive yourself to be capable of. Your vision is personal to you in the beginning but through your vision others will see possibility for themselves. Creating protection for your vision is vital. Not being susceptible to the threat that others face is the main goal of gaining immunity. Look for where others have missed the mark. Not being in-tune with the society and looking for the gap to be filled. Share you vision but expect haters, stay the course no matter what. Remember that's all that matters, is the results, it not how you start but how you finish. Once you have established immunity share it with others who are willing adopt it, as well.

Immunity Quick Guide:

1. Clean your dwelling (house/ apartment) get rid of any clutter. This will create a clearing for the things you desire to show up in your life.

2. Remove anything that no longer matters.

Financial immunity: clear old junk mail. Get a credit report. Make an agreement with all outstanding creditors. Trim down credit card debit but don't get rid of it. Look for hidden value in things you consider trash. All pennies add up. Look for memberships you no longer use. Get up one hour early to work on your vision.

To add to your Health immunity: Get rid of food that has no nutritional value for example process foods/ junk food. All food that goes into your body must have a "why" to serve nutrition as value to your body. Hydration is King. Exercise is a must but Nutrition is 80% of the battle.

3. Create what is possible in your life and see it through. Get a Life Coach to ensure accountability to give you the advantage.

4. Work towards the results you desire daily and don't stop until the results are measured to your satisfaction.

5. Plant positive seeds of growth in others. Create excitement for what is possible in the lives of others and watch it grow. This will add to your own growth by ensuring re-implantation if necessary and building a strong immune system.

The formula to immunity is:

1. Be Aware

2. Take Action

3. Stick to the Plan

4. Follow it through

5. Share the benefits of immunity with others

I hope you found this helpful in leading you onto your road to success. Building Health and Financial Immunity will give you peace of mind when others are living in uncertainty. Be sure you to join the Go Life Coach Family, visit www.golifecoach.com for updated information and receive our mailing list to get alerts on new products and services.

This book comes with a separate 90-day program and one free Coaching session; this is a step by step program where I literally hold your hand to help you to reach your success. This program will aid you in developing Financial Immunity to secure your future. With the loom of another Financial Crisis around the corner you can't afford to not prepare now.

www.ingramcontent.com/pod-product-compliance
Lightning Source LLC
Chambersburg PA
CBHW061229180526
45170CB00003B/1219